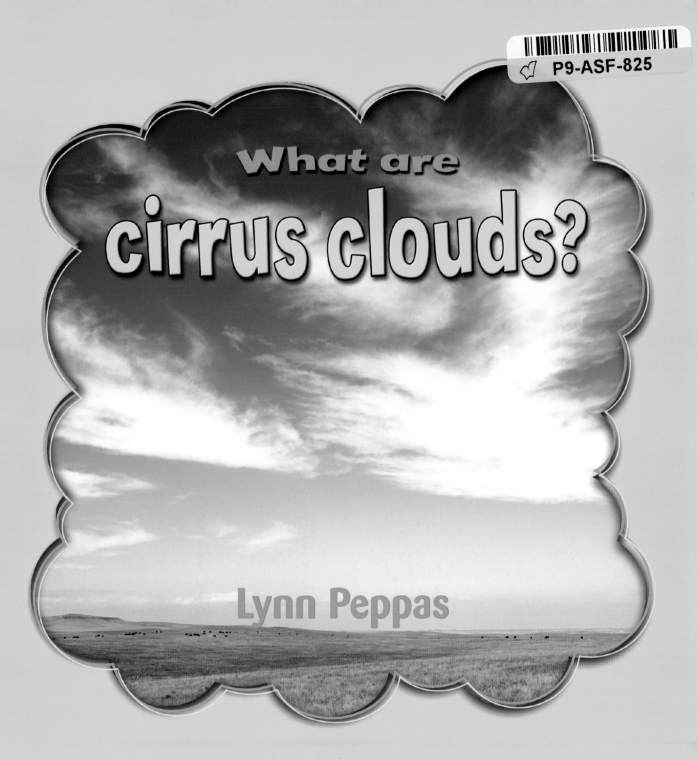

What are cirrus clouds?

Lynn Peppas

Clouds
Close-Up

Author
Lynn Peppas

Publishing plan research and development
Sean Charlebois, Reagan Miller
Crabtree Publishing Company

Editorial director
Kathy Middleton

Editor
Reagan Miller

Proofreader
Crystal Sikkens

Photo research
Allison Napier, Samara Parent

Design
Samara Parent

**Production coordinator
and prepress technician**
Samara Parent

Print coordinator
Katherine Berti

Illustrations
Barbara Bedell: pages 6–7 (except water droplets)
Katherine Bert: page 7 (water droplets)

Photographs
Shutterstock.com: cover, pages 5, 8, 9 (both), 12 (bottom), 13, 15,
    16 (bottom), 17, 19, 23 (both), 24 (all)
Thinkstock.com: title page, contents page, pages 4, 10, 12 (top),
    16 (top), 18, 20, 21
Wikimedia: ©Fir0002, flagstaffotos.com.au: page 14

Library and Archives Canada Cataloguing in Publication

Peppas, Lynn
    What are cirrus clouds? / Lynn Peppas.

(Clouds close-up)
Includes index.
Issued also in electronic format.
ISBN 978-0-7787-4473-3 (bound).--ISBN 978-0-7787-4478-8 (pbk.)

    1. Cirrus clouds--Juvenile literature. 2. Weather--Juvenile literature.
I. Title. II. Series: Peppas, Lynn. Clouds close-up.

QC921.43.C57P47 2012   j551.57'6   C2012-901514-8

Library of Congress Cataloging-in-Publication Data

Peppas, Lynn.
    What are cirrus clouds? / Lynn Peppas.
p. cm. -- (Clouds close-up)
Audience: 5-8
Audience: K to grade 3
Includes index.

ISBN 978-0-7787-4473-3 (reinforced lib. bdg. : alk. paper) -- ISBN 978-0-7787-
4478-8 (pbk. : alk. paper) -- ISBN 978-1-4271-7849-7 (electronic PDF.) -- ISBN
978-1-4271-7964-7 (electronic HTML.)
1. Cirrus clouds--Juvenile literature. 2. Clouds--Juvenile literature. I. Title.

QC921.43.C57P47 2012
551.57'6--dc23
                                        2012008270

Crabtree Publishing Company
www.crabtreebooks.com   1-800-387-7650

Printed in the U.S.A./102012/SN20120907

Published in Canada
Crabtree Publishing
616 Welland Ave.
St. Catharines, Ontario
L2M 5V6

Published in the United States
Crabtree Publishing
PMB 59051
350 Fifth Avenue, 59th Floor
New York, New York 10118

Published in the United Kingdom
Crabtree Publishing
Maritime House
Basin Road North, Hove
BN41 1WR

Published in Australia
Crabtree Publishing
3 Charles Street
Coburg North
VIC 3058

Contents

What are clouds?

A cloud is a large group of water **droplets**. Each droplet is so small and light that it floats in the air. Clouds are pushed by the **wind**. Wind is air moving near Earth's surface.

Crazy for clouds

Clouds have different colors, shapes, and sizes. They form at different heights in the sky. In fact, no two clouds are the same! Different kinds of clouds bring different kinds of **weather**.

What kind of weather will these clouds bring?

5

The water cycle

The **water cycle** describes the movement of water on, in, and above the earth. Clouds are an important part of this cycle. This picture shows how water moves through the cycle.

*Water vapor floats up into the air. It cools and **condenses**, or changes into water droplets. Millions of water droplets join together to form a cloud.*

The Sun heats the water in oceans, lakes, rivers, and even puddles!

*The Sun's heat makes some of the water **evaporate**, or change into **water vapor**.*

water droplets

Water falls from the clouds as **precipitation**.

Moving and changing

Clouds are always moving and changing. Cool air changes water vapor into water droplets and creates clouds. When warm air touches a cloud, the water droplets turn back into water vapor. This causes the cloud to disappear right before your eyes!

These clouds are getting thinner and thinner. Soon they will disappear.

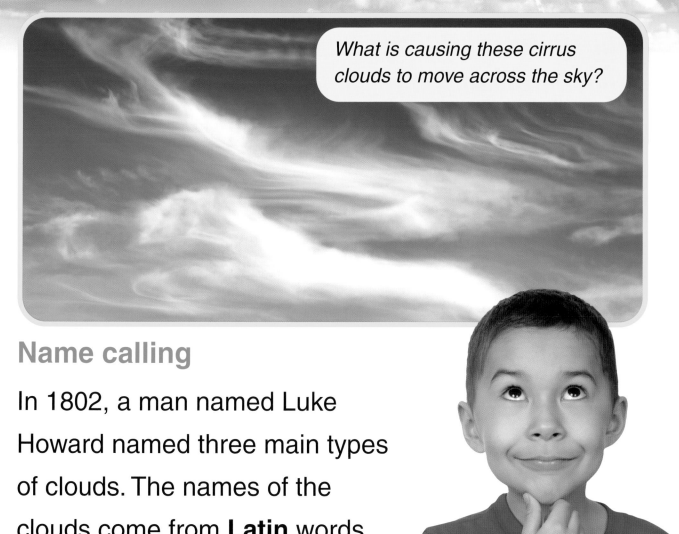

What is causing these cirrus clouds to move across the sky?

Name calling

In 1802, a man named Luke Howard named three main types of clouds. The names of the clouds come from **Latin** words that describe the cloud's shape. They are cumulus, cirrus, and stratus clouds.

How high?

Clouds form at different heights in the sky. Some clouds form high in the sky. Other clouds form low in the sky. There are three words used to describe the height of a cloud in the sky. They are strato, alto, and cirro.

Cloud levels

High clouds

Cloud names that begin with "cirro" are the highest clouds in the sky.

above 18,000 feet (5,486 meters)

Middle clouds

Clouds in the middle of the sky have names that start with "alto."

6,500 feet (1,981 meters) to 18,000 feet (5,486 meters)

Low clouds

Clouds that form low in the sky have "strato" in their names.

up to 6,500 feet (1,981 meters)

Cloud types

High clouds

cirrus
cirrostratus
cirrocumulus

Middle clouds

altostratus
altocumulus

Low clouds

stratus
stratocumulus
nimbostratus

Stratus and cumulus clouds

In Latin, the word stratus means "layers." Stratus clouds cover the sky like layers of gray blankets. They are the lowest clouds in the sky. Sometimes stratus clouds make **drizzle**, or light rain. Rain is a kind of precipitation. Precipitation is water that falls from clouds, such as rain or snow.

Cumulus clouds

Cumulus clouds are puffy white clouds with rounded tops and flat bottoms. The word cumulus means "heap" or "pile" in Latin. These clouds look like piles of cotton balls in the sky. There is a lot of blue sky between different clouds. Cumulus clouds form when the weather is fair and sunny.

What are cirrus clouds?

Sometimes cirrus clouds are called mares' tails. A mare is a female horse.

Cirrus clouds are white and wispy with feathery edges. The word cirrus means "curl of hair" in Latin. Cirrus clouds look like thin bits of curly hair. Cirrus clouds form very high in the sky. They form above the height that most airplanes fly!

Cirrus weather

When you see cirrus clouds, the weather is usually nice and sunny. But watch out for later! Sometimes these clouds are a sign that the weather will change in about a day.

A large number of cirrus clouds may appear before stormy weather.

C-c-cold cirrus clouds

Cirrus clouds are the highest clouds in the sky. They form over six miles (10 kilometers) from Earth's surface. The **temperature** of the air at that height is very cold. Cirrus clouds are made up of **ice crystals** because their water droplets freeze so high in the sky.

ice crystals

Shaped by the wind

The wind is very strong high up where cirrus clouds form. Strong winds pull ice crystals away from the cloud. This is what gives cirrus clouds their feathery edges.

The shape of cirrus clouds tells what direction the wind is blowing.

Cirrostratus clouds

Cirrostratus clouds are high stratus clouds. They cover the sky like a thin, white sheet. These clouds are so thin you can often see the Sun or Moon through the cloud. Cirrostratus clouds create a **halo** around the Sun or Moon. This happens when light from the Sun or Moon passes through cirrostratus clouds.

Cirrostratus weather clues

We often see cirrostratus clouds before rain or a snowstorm. Cirrostratus clouds are a sign that rain or a snowstorm could happen in the next 12 to 24 hours.

Cirrocumulus clouds

Cirrocumulus clouds are high cumulus clouds. They look like patches of wavy, little clouds. Sometimes the waves form in rows. Cirrocumulus clouds are also called "mackerel sky" because they look like the pattern on the scales of a fish.

Cirrocumulus weather

Cirrocumulus clouds usually form in winter during cold, sunny days. They mean that good weather is coming within one day's time.

Make your own cloud journal

Directions:

1. Each morning for a week go outside and **observe**, or look at, the clouds.

2. In a notebook, label one page for each day of the week, from Sunday to Saturday.

3. Draw a picture of the clouds you see in the sky. Ask yourself these questions as you are drawing.

What shape are they?

How high are they in the sky?

What color are they?

Is there more than one kind of cloud in the sky?

Monday

Tuesday

4. Weather report. Look at your observations and decide what kind of weather you think the day will bring.

Words to know

condense To change from a gas to a liquid
drizzle A light, misty rain
droplet A tiny drop of water
evaporate To change from a liquid to a gas
halo A circle of light that surrounds something
ice crystal A small piece of ice that floats in the air in cold weather
Latin An old language that was used thousands of years ago
observe To study or look at
precipitation Rain, snow, or hail that falls from clouds to the earth
temperature A degree of heat or cold
water cycle Describes how water moves between Earth's surface and the sky
water vapor Water that has changed from a liquid to a gas
weather What the air is like at a certain time and place
wind Naturally moving air

Index

Learning more

Books:
What is Climate? by Bobbie Kalman. Crabtree Publishing Company, 2012.
Changing Weather: Storms by Bobbie Kalman. Crabtree Publishing Company, 2006.
The Weather by Deborah Chancellor. Crabtree Publishing Company, 2010.

Websites:
http://eo.ucar.edu/webweather/cloudhome.html
www.weatherwizkids.com
www.northcanton.sparcc.org/~elem/interactivities/clouds/cloudsread.html